LITTLE BIGFOOT GOES TO CAMP

Liz Berry Wells

Copyright © 2023 Liz Berry Wells

All Rights Reserved

First Edition

Table of Contents

Chapter 1 3

Chapter 2 7

Chapter 3 11

Chapter 4 15

Chapter 5 19

Chapter 6 23

Chapter 7 27

Chapter 1

There once was a family of Bigfoots that lived in the forest. There was a dad,mom, and baby Bigfoot. Life was good for them. This family was different from most Bigfoot families... they bathed regularly and smelled like sweet cedar and fresh mountain breeze. The parents adored their son and taught him how to hunt and most importantly: to hide from humans!

The forest offered many things for a baby Bigfoot to do. He could swing from trees, splash in the water and play hide and go seek with his parents. But he had rules to follow to be safe. He could only stay in the deepest part of the forest where the trees were so dense that hiding was easy, food was plentiful, and they were far away from humans!

Chapter 2

When he was 2 years old Little Bigfoot started Bigfoot Camp. His family had to travel a great distance to get to the camp. When they got there, he saw Bigfoots his own age who were as curious and playful as he was. All the parents stayed for the weekend and then they left to hunt and to survey the land.

The camp was run by two older bigfoots: one male and one female. They looked to be around 20 years old. The female, Lucy, over saw hut building and team building. Her dark, kind eyes shined brightly against her reddish, rough fur. The male, Rusty, lived up to his name. From his rustic features (raggedy brown/black hair, and his large wide face with inquisitive black eyes) to his height. Some said he was the tallest bigfoot that ever lived. That by himself made him a formidable creature! He was in charge of hunting and hiding from humans.

The camp itself was surrounded by a dense forest. The tall pine trees swayed in time with the wind. A waterfall could be heard off in the distance. Little Bigfoot thought this was the most beautiful place he had ever seen!

The students stayed in huts built by other Bigfoots. Little Bigfoot had a roommate named Musky, due to his smell. He smelled like a mixture of garlic, fish, spicy and fragrant perfume. They hit it off right off the bat and did everything together. Now Musky was very tall for his age, and no one EVER messed with him. Little Bigfoot and Musky had the same classes except for hut making. Everything was alright for Little Bigfoot if Musky was around. When he wasn't—that was a different story.

Chapter 3

Little Bigfoot was such a friendly, caring Bigfoot. He would go out of his way to help anyone with any task. But that just seemed to make things worse. He would be bullied anytime Musky wasn't there to defend him. Some of the bigfoots called him names like Daisy and Wimpy because he was so clean and nice. During hut making class they would hide his tools when the teacher wasn't looking. He would be sent to detention when it was time for recess. He tried time and again to tell Lucy what really happened, but she dismissed him, telling him he must take responsibility for his actions.

Soon, Little Bigfoot started withdrawing and staying to himself. He wouldn't go sit by the fire for story time at the end of the day.

Musky tried to get him to join in, but he would just sit in their hut crying. Finally, Little Bigfoot had had enough, he knew what he had to do.

Chapter 4

That night he waited until everyone was asleep in their huts and until he could hear the gentle snores of Musky. He quietly slipped out of his hut and surveyed the campsite to see which way he should start moving. He decided to move in an Easterly direction away from camp. He first started walking and then, when he felt he was far enough away, he started running as fast as lightning. He had to get away from this place that caused him so much pain. He would miss Musky, but he would be better off without him. In fact, everyone would be better off without him. Those thoughts kept racing through his mind. Before he knew it the forest was not as dense. He could see pockets of trails and even big dwellings he had never seen before. Then he smelled a smell he had never smelt before. And heard sounds he had never heard before: COULD IT BE HUMANS?

Chapter 5

Little Bigfoot spied the last big tree he could find and quickly dashed behind it for cover. While he caught his breath and began to think of a plan. He realized that he was not too far from what looked like a human dwelling. All he needed to do was wait until the humans awoke and came outside: then he would make himself visible to them. After that he didn't know what would happen to him and he didn't care either.

When Little Bigfoot found the tree, it was dawn. He hadn't realized how tired he was from running. He fell in to a deep sleep. When he awoke it must have been around noon, looking at the sun. He gathered all the courage he could muster and peered around the tree. He saw a man loading something large into a contraption that had doors in front and a long flat space with a gate at the back. He also saw a younger human that was much smaller but seemed strong as he was loading things into the back of this contraption as well.

    Little Bigfoot thought it was now or never. He was about to step into the light when a big hand grabbed him from behind.

Chapter 6

Frightened, Little Bigfoot turned around. To his relief he saw his counselor, Lucy. Lucy put a finger to her mouth and led him quietly towards the camp. After they had gotten far enough away from the humans Lucy began to talk. She asked why he would do something so foolish as to nearly get himself killed.

Didn't he know the whole camp was worried sick about him. He told her that not everyone was. He went onto tell her about all the bullying that went on. Lucy's eyes filled with tears.

She had no idea this was going on and she felt ashamed. She apologized to him for not listening to him and said she would do much better.

Once they finally reached camp, Musky was the first to greet him with a great big hug. When everyone arrived back at camp, they all gathered around the fire. Lucy and Rusty lead a discussion regarding the bullying of Little Bigfoot. They needed the ones responsible to come forward as it was nearly fatal for Little Bigfoot. The ones responsible reluctantly raised their hands and apologized to Little Bigfoot for picking on him. He asked them why they did it. Most of them said they were just following the crowd. Some said they really didn't know. The leader of the bullies said he did it because it was fun. Now Lucy did not like this answer and angerly pulled him aside and said, "This was not fun! This was pathetic!

Your parents are coming to pick you up tomorrow and they will be hearing about what you did!"

Chapter 7

That night Musky and Little Bigfoot stayed up late talking and laughing. He was so glad that Lucy saved him. He realized that people really did care about him and that if there ever was a next time, he would try harder to talk to the adult in charge to let them know what was going on.

The next morning everyone was packed up and ready to go when their parents showed up there were hugs all around. Rusty told Little Bigfoot's parents about the bullying and what happened. They were so grateful to

Lucy for finding him. Lucy was talking with the head bully's parents, and they did not look happy.

Musky and Little Bigfoot made plans to visit each other in the next few months. They all went on their way home. As for Little Bigfoot, he smiled the whole way home.

Made in the USA
Columbia, SC
26 April 2025